Choctaw Mythology

Captivating Myths from the Choctaw and Other Indigenous Peoples from the Southeastern United States

© Copyright 2020

All Rights Reserved. No part of this book may be reproduced in any form without permission in writing from the author. Reviewers may quote brief passages in reviews.

Disclaimer: No part of this publication may be reproduced or transmitted in any form or by any means, mechanical or electronic, including photocopying or recording, or by any information storage and retrieval system, or transmitted by email without permission in writing from the publisher.

While all attempts have been made to verify the information provided in this publication, neither the author nor the publisher assumes any responsibility for errors, omissions or contrary interpretations of the subject matter herein.

This book is for entertainment purposes only. The views expressed are those of the author alone, and should not be taken as expert instruction or commands. The reader is responsible for his or her own actions.

Adherence to all applicable laws and regulations, including international, federal, state and local laws governing professional licensing, business practices, advertising and all other aspects of doing business in the US, Canada, UK or any other jurisdiction is the sole responsibility of the purchaser or reader.

Neither the author nor the publisher assumes any responsibility or liability whatsoever on the behalf of the purchaser or reader of these materials. Any perceived slight of any individual or organization is purely unintentional.

Free Bonus from Captivating History (Available for a Limited time)

Hi History Lovers!

Now you have a chance to join our exclusive history list so you can get your first history ebook for free as well as discounts and a potential to get more history books for free! Simply visit the link below to join.

Captivatinghistory.com/ebook

Also, make sure to follow us on Facebook, Twitter and Youtube by searching for Captivating History.

Contents

INTRODUCTION 1
PART I: CHOCTAW MYTHS AND LEGENDS..4
PART II: LEGENDS FROM OTHER SOUTHERN TRIBES..........................22
HERE'S ANOTHER BOOK BY MATT CLAYTON THAT YOU MIGHT LIKE 40
FREE BONUS FROM CAPTIVATING HISTORY (AVAILABLE FOR A LIMITED TIME) 41
BIBLIOGRAPHY..42

Introduction

When people think about Native Americans, the images that most likely spring to mind are Plains tribes or the desert southwest, and not those of the southeastern states. This perception is largely the result of history and white storytelling practices. White incursions into southeastern indigenous territory coupled with the forcible relocation of peoples from that region, demanded by the Removal Act of 1830, pushed these people onto reservations and out of the public consciousness, while Western films and television shows mostly focus on white settlement of the Western United States and the resulting conflict between whites and Plains tribes. However, these skewed views do not represent modern reality. Many southeastern tribes affected by the Removal Act still exist—as do other tribes throughout the United States—yet their cultures were irreparably damaged by the genocidal policies of the white state and federal governments.

Before the disruption of southeastern indigenous cultures by white settlers, the southeastern region's indigenous peoples relied on a combination of agriculture, hunting, and gathering for their sustenance. Due to their reliance on agriculture—primarily the cultivation of corn (maize), squash, and beans (the so-called "three sisters")—these tribes were sedentary, living in towns and villages that consisted of dwellings, storehouses, and a townhouse, the latter of which was the venue for councils and other important group activities.

Some of the southeastern tribes are descendants of the ancient Mississippian culture, part of whose legacy is several large mounds found in various places throughout the Mississippi Valley. The Choctaw were among these mound-builders; the story of Nanih Waiya told in this volume is a mythical relation of the origin of that particular mound, which still stands today in Winston County, Mississippi, and which in 2008 was formally ceded to the Mississippi Band of Choctaw Indians. These mounds were used as ceremonial or religious sites in some cases, while others appear to have been constructed over burials.

Many southeast peoples speak languages in the Muskogean language family, and many myths and tales also have versions that are shared among tribes. Rabbit is a trickster hero in all of these cultures, while other animals common to the region, such as turkeys and alligators, make appearances as well. Thunder beings appear in tales from both the Choctaw and Natchez peoples—only the Choctaw story is presented in this volume—while the owl acts as a villain in stories from both the Choctaw and the Caddo.

The first part of this book contains Choctaw myths and legends. In this section are stories that explain Choctaw beliefs about the origin and structure of the universe and the origin of corn, an important staple food. The alligator appears here not as a villain but as a grateful recipient of human aid, while the owl is a murderous old woman. Adventurers seek new places in the Choctaw migration legend and in the story of Tashka and Walo, two boys who journey to the home of the Sun.

The second half of the book comprises stories from six other southeastern tribes: the Seminole, Natchez, Alabama, Creek, Caddo, and Chitimacha. Animal characters such as Alligator, Rabbit, and Owl play roles here, too, the first in a just-so story about the shape of the alligator's snout, the second in his usual guise as a wily trickster, and the third as a devious man who dupes two ambitious girls into becoming his wives. Journeys to the sky country are represented by the tale of the sky maidens who come down to Earth to play ball, and in the story of the gifts of Kutnahin, a solar deity of the Chitimacha people.

Tie-snakes, which appear in a Creek legend presented below, are supernatural water-dwelling serpents that play a role in many southeastern legends and can be benevolent or malevolent. Here they are helpful, provided that the hero of the story can meet their demands. The other Creek story in this volume relies on the common folklore tropes of the man-eating beast and the child-prodigy hero, who is the only one who can defeat the villain. But regardless of the origin of the story, whether from the Choctaw, the Creek, or any of the other tribes represented here, each tale in this volume explains something important about indigenous peoples' understanding of the world and the places of the people, animals, and birds who live in it.

Part I: Choctaw Myths and Legends

The Creation of the World

When the world was new, all that existed was a flat plain and the sky above it. On the plain was a great hill called Nanih Waiya, "the sloping hill."

The Creator decided that the world needed some people, so he caused people to come out of the earth around the mound. Each person that emerged went and sat on the hill. Some say that the first people to emerge were the Muskogee, who left and went east, where they made their home. Allegedly, the Cherokees and Chickasaws came next. The Cherokees followed the Muskogees' trail, but the Muskogees had stopped to smoke tobacco on the way and accidentally caused a fire in the forest. The Cherokees could not find the Muskogees' trail, which had been burned away by the fire, so they turned north and made their home there. The Chickasaws followed the Cherokees and made their home nearby. Then the Choctaws came out of the mound, but they decided to stay right there, and so they made their home next to Nanih Waiya.

The Creator watched all the people come out of the mound and go their different ways, and when he thought the world had enough people, he stamped hard on the ground with his foot. Some people were still being formed when he did this, still coming out of the earth, but when the Creator stamped his foot, they stopped being created and died, sinking back into the ground.

The Creator gathered the people on the hill and told them that they would live forever.

"What is 'forever'? Is living forever a good thing? What happens to us when forever is over?" the people asked.

The Creator became annoyed that the people did not understand what a great gift he was offering them, so he made them mortal instead, and this is why we have death.

After the Creator made the people, a great flood came. The waters rushed and flowed all around the mound where the people were sitting. The wind blew in great gusts, causing waves to form on the waters. Soon the storm and the flood were over, and the people saw that the land was no longer a flat plain with their mound in the middle. Instead, there were hills, mountains, valleys, and riverbeds and streambeds with good, fresh water.

"I am going to make some plants now," the Creator said. "I will show you which ones will give you good things to eat."

Then the Creator made many kinds of trees. Among them were the hickory, the chestnut, and the oak. The Creator showed the people the nuts made by the hickory and the chestnut and the acorns made by the oak. He told them that these would be their food.

Another legend says that the Creator did not bring the people forth from the mud of the earth but rather from a great cavern that lay beneath the mound of Nanih Waiyah. At the same time that the Creator formed the people, he also made the grasshoppers, and both people and grasshoppers climbed out of the cavern together. But then the mother of all the grasshoppers was killed by one of the people, and so no more grasshoppers came out of the cavern.

The people were also very careless of the grasshoppers, who shared the earth with them after they came out of the cavern. Sometimes the people stepped on the grasshoppers, crushing them to death. Although no more new grasshoppers were being created, ever more people were emerging from the cavern, and soon the grasshoppers became frightened that they would all be trampled to death.

"O Creator!" the grasshoppers cried. "Look at how the people trample on us! Please stop making more people, or there will be no more grasshoppers left!"

The Creator heard the grasshoppers' prayer and closed the cavern's mouth so that no more people could come out. The Creator turned the many people who were still inside the cavern into ants. This is why ants live underground but sometimes crawl out of their holes to walk around on the earth's surface.

The Building of Nanih Waiya

The sacred hill of Nanih Waiya has stood at the heart of Choctaw lands for so long that some say it was there from the time the world was made and that Nanih Waiya is the place from which the people emerged when the Creator first made the world. However, others tell a different story. They say that Nanih Waiya is a thing made by human hands and that the story of the Choctaw people begins in a land far, far away, in the west of the world.

Long ago—or so these people say—the Choctaw lived far away in the west. But their lives were uneasy because their neighbors were very warlike and gave the Choctaw no peace. The people held a council to decide what to do. In the end, the chief appointed two brothers, Chahtah and Chikasah, to lead the people to a new place where they would be safe.

That evening, the medicine man made a sacred pole and planted it in the earth in the middle of the village.

"This pole will tell us which way we should go," the medicine man said. "In the morning, we will look at the pole and go in the direction it is pointing."

In the morning, the people looked at the pole and saw that it was pointing toward the east. The people packed their belongings and began the long journey eastward. The medicine man brought the pole with him, and every night he planted it in the ground where the people were encamped. Every morning, the pole would be found leaning to the east, and so the people continued their journey eastward.

For many weeks and many months, the people walked and walked, with the pole always pointing to the east every morning. This went on until they came to the banks of a great river. None of the people had ever seen a river that wide.

"What are we to do?" they asked. "Are we to cross and continue our journey? We have never crossed a river like that before."

The medicine man said, "We will camp here tonight, and in the morning, we will see what the sacred pole tells us to do."

In the morning, the pole was pointing to the east, telling the people they must cross the river. The people made rafts and canoes. They boarded these craft with their belongings, and so crossed the great river. On the eastern bank of the river, the people resumed their journey because that is what the pole had told them to do. After a very long day's walk, they made camp, and in the morning, they looked at the pole to see where they must go next, but they found the pole was standing upright, just as the medicine man had planted it the night before.

"This means that this is the place where we are to live," the medicine man said.

To celebrate their arrival in their new home, the people built a great mound, and this is how Nanih Waiyah was made.

The people lived near Nanih Waiyah peacefully for many years, but soon the brothers, Chahtah and Chikasah, had a falling out.

"One of us needs to leave," Chahtah said.

"Yes," Chikasah said. "But how shall we decide which one?"

They went to the medicine man for help.

The medicine man said, "One of you shall stand there, and the other there. I shall place the pole between you. I will let go of the pole, and whoever the pole points to when it falls is the one who must leave."

The brothers agreed that this would be the solution, and when the pole was dropped, it pointed to Chikasah. Chikasah and his followers then packed up their belongings and moved to the north.

The Hunters and the Unknown Woman

Once two hunters had tried for two days to catch something to bring back to their families, with no success. They were now at the end of the second day, and the only thing to show for their efforts was one black hawk, which they had shot earlier that day. The hawk certainly was not enough to bring home for their families. It wasn't even really enough for the two of them, but they plucked it and set it over a fire to cook anyway since they had no other food and they were very hungry after a hard day's work.

The two men sat next to the fire waiting for their dinner to be ready. They did not speak to one another but rather sat lost in their thoughts and feeling sad about their lack of success. Just as the full moon began to rise, they heard a low, plaintive sound.

"What was that?" the first hunter asked.

"Sounded like a dove of some kind," the second replied.

"Maybe."

They sat by the fire a little longer as the moon rose into the sky. When the moon was high enough in the sky to cover everything in silvery light, the sound happened again, except this time, it was much louder and closer.

"Did you hear that? It is that sound again," the first hunter said. "It's getting closer. I think we ought to go and see what it is."

The second hunter agreed.

They went to the nearby riverbank but did not see anything along it or across it. However, when they turned around to go back to their camp, a young woman was standing on a small mound before them. She was dressed all in white clothing and very beautiful.

"Do you have anything to eat?" the woman asked the hunters. "I am very hungry indeed."

"We do not have much," the second hunter said, "but what we have, you are welcome to share."

The hunters brought the roasted hawk over to the mound and gave it to the woman. She ate some of it and gave the rest back to the hunters.

"Thank you," she said. "I was nearly dead of hunger, but you saved me. I will never forget your kindness. One month from now, return to this spot, and you will find a gift waiting for you."

Then the woman vanished, her form dissipating on the breeze.

In the morning, the hunters returned to their village, still sadly empty-handed. They did not tell anyone about the woman they had met, because they knew she was a very important and powerful being: the daughter of the Great Spirit.

The days passed, and the hunters returned to the mound on the day the woman had told them to be there. They waited and waited, but the woman did not appear. Soon it was nightfall, and the full moon was rising over the river, just as it had done on the day they had met the woman.

"I don't think she is coming," the first hunter said.

"She promised, though," the second said. "Maybe we are waiting in the wrong place. Maybe we're supposed to be waiting on the mound where we first saw her."

The hunters then went to the mound, and when they got to the top, they saw that it was covered with many tall plants. The leaves were long and flat, and growing on the stalks were long pods with silky tassels peeking out of the ends.

"What do we do with this?" the first hunter asked.

"Maybe it is something to eat. We gave her food when she was hungry, so maybe she's repaying us in kind," the second replied.

The second hunter picked one of the long pods and stripped away the leafy outer covering. He pulled off the strands of silk that lay along the rows between the kernels and took a bite.

"Oh, this is very good!" he said. "We must bring this back to the people. We can plant this, and then we will always have food right there in our village. We'll never be hungry again!"

The two hunters gathered as much corn as possible and brought it back to their village. They told the people how they had come by it. The people were all astonished and rejoiced that such a precious gift should have been given to them.

And this is how the Choctaws first got corn.

The Hunter and the Alligator

One winter, the village hunters all went out to see whether they might get some deer to bring home. All the hunters but one successfully brought down some fine deer, which they took back to their village. However, one hunter was not so lucky. He tried shooting the deer he saw, but every arrow went amiss. He wandered in the forest for three days and caught nothing to bring home.

Near the end of the third day, he decided to give up and go back to his village.

No sooner had he started his journey than he heard an strange, raspy voice say, "Please help me."

The hunter looked around but could not see anyone.

He turned back to his path home, but then the voice said, "Please, do not leave me here. I'll die. Help me."

"Where are you?" the hunter asked.

"Over here."

The hunter went toward the sound of the voice, and soon he came across an alligator. The alligator looked very ill and weak, with very dry skin.

"Please help me," the alligator said. "I need to get to water soon, or I will die. Is there any water nearby?"

"Oh, yes," the hunter replied. "There is a nice river off that way, through the forest."

"Can you carry me there? I am too weak and sick to walk all that way myself."

"No, I don't think I should do that."

"I will not eat you. I won't even bite. Not one little nibble. Just please, please carry me to the water, or I will surely die."

The hunter looked at the alligator, and although he felt very sorry for it, he still was not sure whether he could trust the animal's word. But then he hit upon an idea.

"I will carry you on one condition," the hunter said.

"Name it," the alligator said.

"You must let me tie up your feet so that your claws cannot scratch me. And you must let me tie up your mouth, so you can't bite me."

"That is fair. I promise I won't bite or scratch."

The hunter cut some vines, and with some of them, he tied the alligator's jaws tight shut. Then he tied the alligator's feet. The alligator made no protest at all; it just lay there patiently while the hunter tied it up.

"There," the hunter said. "Now, I will carry you to the river. I'll untie you when we get there. I expect you to keep your word that you won't hurt me because if you try, I'll have to kill you, and I'd rather not do that."

The alligator made a noise that the hunter took for assent and then hoisted the animal up onto his shoulders and walked to the river. At the riverbank, he gently put the alligator down and cut the bonds on its feet and mouth with his knife. True to its word, the alligator did not try to bite or scratch but rather slithered into the water. It dove beneath the surface and then came up again. It dove and surfaced three more times and then went down again and stayed down for a long time. Just as the hunter was about to turn to go home, the alligator came back up.

"Wait!" the alligator said. "You saved my life. I cannot let you leave without a gift. I see that you have been out hunting. If you do what I say, you will never return home empty-handed, and your family will always have plenty to eat. Go into the forest, and when you see a small doe, do not shoot it. Next, you will see a large doe and then a small buck, but do not shoot either of them. Last you will see a very large buck. Shoot it and bring it home to your village."

Then the alligator slid back into the water, and the hunter never saw it again.

The hunter started on his journey back home, hunting as he went. He saw a small doe, but he did not shoot it. Then he saw a large doe, but he did not shoot it either. Not long afterward, he saw a small buck, but he let that one go too. Finally, he came across a large buck. He nocked an arrow to the string and took a shot. The deer went down, killed instantly. The hunter brought the buck home, and from that day forward, he never returned to his village empty-handed, and his family always had plenty to eat.

The Boys Who Followed the Sun

Once there were twin brothers named Tashka and Walo. They were very curious about the world around them and always wanted to know more. When they were about four years old, they began to watch the Sun as it rose in the east, moved across the sky, and set in the west.

They went to their mother and said, "Mother, where does the Sun go at night?"

"Nobody knows," their mother replied. "I was always told that the Sun dies when it sets and is born again when it rises in the morning."

Soon the boys could talk of nothing other than where the Sun went every night. They asked many people, but none gave the boys a satisfactory answer.

One day, Tashka and Walo watched the Sun rise and move across the sky, as they had been doing for some time, but when it set that night, they said to one another, "Let us follow the Sun. We will see for ourselves where it goes at night."

Off they went, even though they were only four years old.

For many days, they followed the Sun through country they knew very well, but still, they came no closer to the place where the Sun went to die. They kept traveling through country they did not know at all, but even though they traveled very far every day, they still came no closer to the Sun's home.

The boys traveled day after day, year after year until they were grown into young men.

Finally, they came to the edge of the land. Before them was a wide sea, so broad that they could not see what lay on the other side.

They sat on the beach to watch the Sun set, and as it did, Tashka said, "I bet the Sun lives over the edge of the sea. If we go there, we will be at his house."

"Yes," Walo said. "We should journey across the sea, too, and if we get to the edge when the Sun does, we can follow him home."

The next morning, the boys built themselves a sturdy canoe, and in the evening, they began paddling across the water.

They arrived at the edge of the sea just as the Sun did, so the boys could follow the Sun into his home.

In the Sun's home, there was a multitude of women. Most of the women were stars, but one woman was the Moon, and she was the Sun's wife.

The Moon saw the boys and said, "How did you come here? Mortal beings do not belong in this house."

"We are Tashka and Walo," the boys said. "We wanted to know where the Sun goes every night. We have been following him, day after day, year after year since we were tiny children."

Then the Sun saw the boys. He said to his wife, "Go and boil a big pot of water."

The Moon did as she was bid, and when the water was boiling, the Sun put the boys into the pot. When they had been in the water a little while, the Sun reached in and rubbed their bodies until their skin came off, and they were red all over.

When the boiling was done, the Sun said, "Now, tell me why you are here. You are still living men, and it is not time for you to join me here in my house."

The boys explained that they had followed him, day after day, year after year because they wanted to see where he died at night.

"That was bravely done," the Sun said, "but you can't stay. I have to send you home now. But listen to me: Once you reach your home, you may not speak to anyone for four days. If you speak before the four days are over, you will die soon thereafter. If you speak after the four days are over, then you will have long and happy lives."

The Sun then summoned Buzzard. He put Tashka and Walo on Buzzard's back and told him to take the young men home. Buzzard flew up into the sky and wheeled around until he found the right direction to go. Down and down he flew, until he reached the clouds. This part of the journey was easy because above the clouds, there is never any wind. But once Buzzard got below the clouds, a strong wind began to blow him to and fro.

"Hang on tight!" Buzzard said to the young men as he tried to keep them safely on his back.

No matter how hard the wind blew, Buzzard kept flying toward Tashka and Walo's home, and soon the young men were safely on the ground not far from their village. Tashka and Walo bid Buzzard farewell and walked a little way down the path, but they were so shaken from their dangerous flight that they decided to rest awhile under a tree.

While the young men were resting, a man from their village passed by. He saw Tashka and Walo and greeted them, but they did not reply.

"Why won't you speak to me? Are you ill? Have I offended you?" the man asked.

But no matter what the man said, the young men would not answer.

"Oh, well. You don't have to talk if you don't want to, but someone has to tell your mother that you are back. She has been mourning you all these long years and will be so happy to see you again."

Soon Tashka and Walo's mother came running up the path, weeping with joy. She embraced her children and noted what fine young men they had become.

"Where have you been? We looked everywhere for you, for so very long. I missed you terribly, and I am so happy to see you alive again," she said.

The boys did not answer her, for they meant to follow the Sun's instructions. Their mother kept asking question after question, but when the boys remained silent, she became angry. Finally, she forced them to speak.

"We went to see where the Sun dies at night," the young men said. "We journeyed day after day, year after year until we came to the Sun's house. He put us on a buzzard that carried us home, but he also said that we would die soon thereafter if we spoke before four days had passed after our arrival home. That is why we were not answering you."

At this, the mother became very sorrowful. "I should not have forced you to speak. I am sorry for that. But come home now and have a meal, and tell me where you have been and what you have seen."

The young men went home with their mother. She cooked them a fine meal, and they told the story of their adventures to all the village. When their tale was ended, they both lay down on the ground and died. It was then that they went back to the Sun's house, where they have lived ever since.

The Owl Woman

Some children were playing outside their house when they saw someone coming down the path toward their village.

"Who is that?" one child asked.

"I don't know. I've never seen someone like that before," another replied.

"Let's go and see who it is!" a third said, and so off they went to greet the stranger.

However, the children had not gone far when they saw that the stranger was a very old woman. Her body was bent with age, and her hair was white. In her hands, she carried a basket with a lid. She was so old and so bent that the children became frightened and ran back home. But soon, curiosity overcame them, and they went out to greet the old woman, who had arrived in their village at that time.

"Don't be afraid of me," the woman said. "After all, I am your great-great-great-grandmother! You have never seen me because I live very far away. Even your mother has never seen me! But maybe you can go and fetch your mother, and tell her that I have come to visit."

The children did as the old woman bid them, and soon their mother had helped the old woman into the house and given her a deerskin to sit on. The mother and her children prepared a meal and gave it to the woman.

When the woman was done eating, she asked the children, "Tell me about your father. When he is home, where does he sleep?"

The children pointed out the place where their father slept.

That night, when the family was asleep, the old woman went to the place where the father lay and cut off his head. She put the head in her basket and covered the body with a blanket. Then she crept silently out of the house.

In the morning, the mother woke and started about the business of the day. She saw that her husband was still in bed, which was strange because he usually was the first one up.

"Are you ill, husband? Why are you still in bed?" she asked.

When her husband did not answer, the wife pulled off the blanket. She was horrified to find her husband's headless body beneath it.

Meanwhile, the old woman was hastening down the path away from the village, carrying the basket with the man's head in it. After a time, she came across a bear.

"Good morning," the bear said. "What do you have in your basket?"

"Oh, it is something very dangerous indeed. If I show it to you, you will instantly become blind. That's how bad it is," she replied.

The bear was alarmed by this and asked no further questions and went on his way.

The woman continued down the road until she met a deer. The deer also asked what was in the basket, and when the woman warned him that he would go blind if he saw it, the deer asked no further questions and went on his way.

All throughout the day, the woman met animals along the path. They all asked the same question, and she gave them all the same answer. The animals all left the woman alone after she answered them until she came across two wildcats.

"Good day, old woman," the wildcats said. "That's a fine basket you have there. Can we see inside it?"

"Oh, no. I can't show this to anyone. Whoever sees what I have in this basket will go blind instantly," she replied.

"That doesn't matter to us at all," the first wildcat said as he tore the basket out of the woman's hands and lifted the lid.

When the wildcat saw what was inside the basket, he showed it to his friend. Both wildcats were horrified and angered by what they saw.

"We've heard of you, old woman," the first wildcat said.

"Yes, indeed we have," the second said. "You killed some of our friends. Now we shall avenge them."

Then the wildcats leaped at the old woman and took her captive.

While the first wildcat held the old woman, the second went looking for something to use as a weapon to kill her with.

Once the second wildcat was out of earshot, the old woman said to the first, "You know, if you really want to kill me, you should use that tree branch over there. It looks quite solid and probably would make a fine club. Also, it is good luck to kill me. Why wait for your friend to come back and let him have all the luck? You should do it yourself. I think you deserve it more, anyway."

The first wildcat wanted that good luck for himself, so he let the woman go and went to pick up the tree branch. However, when he returned, the woman was gone, for she had turned into an owl and flown far away.

The Hunter Who Became a Deer

A hunter went out early one morning to see whether he might get any game. He spent all day in the forest, but game was scarce, and even when he did spy something, his arrows went astray. As the sun was setting, he came across a beautiful doe. He nocked an arrow to the string and let fly. The arrow found its mark, and the doe collapsed to the ground, dead.

The hunter saw that it was nearly dark, and since he was far from home, he decided to spend the night there and take the carcass home in the morning. When the sun rose, the hunter heard a voice speaking to him.

"Wake up," the voice said.

The hunter sat up, startled. He looked around, and there was the doe he had shot the night before. She was still lying on the ground, but her head was up, and she was looking right at him.

"Don't be afraid," the doe said. "I only want to ask you something. Will you come home with me?"

All the hunter could do was blink in astonishment, so the doe said, "Please come home with me."

The hunter agreed, so the doe got to her feet and began to lead the hunter through the forest.

They traveled a very long way, and soon they were in country that was unfamiliar to the hunter. Finally, they arrived at a place where there was a very large boulder. Underneath the boulder was a hole, and the doe went into it. The hunter followed her, and there before him stood the king of the deer, a huge buck with enormous antlers.

"Welcome. You have traveled a long way. You may rest if you wish," the buck said.

The hunter did not know what to say in reply, so he lay down in the place the buck showed to him and fell fast asleep.

Now, in the cave where the king of the deer lived, there were many piles of deer hooves, antlers, and skins. The buck and the doe selected various hooves and tried to fit them over the man's hands and feet, but it was some time before they found pairs that fit him perfectly. Next, they found a skin and wrapped it around his body. They finished their work by affixing a set of antlers to his head. The hunter slept soundly through all of this, and when he woke, he found that he had been turned into a deer.

He left the cave and went through the forest in deer form, and for a time, lived in the way that deer do.

When the hunter did not return home, his mother became worried. After several days had passed, she asked the village men to help her find her son. She went out with a search party, and after some time, they came across the hunter's bow and arrows, which he had left behind in the place where he had shot the doe. The people gathered around the bow and arrows and began singing together. Before they could finish the song, a herd of deer came bounding through the forest and encircled them. One buck left the circle and walked up to the hunter's mother.

"Hello, Mother. It is I, your son. The king of the deer turned me into a buck. I live with the deer now," the buck said.

All were astonished to hear the deer speak, for it spoke with the voice of the missing hunter. The mother cried out when she heard her son's voice.

"No, no! My son cannot be a deer. Take that deerskin off him," she said to the men of the search party. "I don't want to have a deer for a son. Take off the skin and the hooves and the antlers."

"Wait! Please don't remove my skin. I have become a deer, and if you do what you suggest, I will surely die," the buck said.

"No matter. I will not have a deer for a son. I'd rather you were dead," the hunter's mother said.

At that, the men grabbed the buck and began flaying off its skin, but what the buck had said was true; he had become a deer indeed, and so he died at the hands of the men from his village.

When the buck was dead, the men carried it back to the village, where the hunter's mother told everyone what had happened. Then the people buried the deer with great care, holding a sacred dance as part of the ceremony.

Part II: Legends from Other Southern Tribes

How Alligator's Nose Was Broken (*Seminole*)

One day, the animals decided to challenge the birds to a ball game. The birds agreed. Alligator was the captain of the animals' team, and Eagle was the captain of the birds' team. They found a good place to have the game and set up goalposts at either end. The medicine men for each team cast spells on the ball, hoping that this would help their team win.

Finally, it was time for the game to start. Each team gathered under its goalpost, while animals and birds for miles around stood around the perimeter of the field to watch the action. The game began when the ball was tossed into the air.

Alligator got there first and snatched up the ball in his strong jaws. He started running directly for the goal. He was so fast and so strong that none of the birds could take the ball away from him. Alligator's wife jumped up and down on the sidelines, cheering for her husband.

"That is my son's father!" she shouted. "He is the fastest and the strongest! Look at him go!"

Just as Alligator was nearing the goal, Eagle swooped down from high above the field. He swooped down so hard and so fast that when he hit Alligator in the nose, Alligator yelped with pain and almost dropped the ball. When Alligator opened his mouth to yell, Turkey ran in and, paying no mind to Alligator's sharp teeth, snatched up the ball and ran toward his goalposts. He got there before any of the animals could catch him and tossed the ball between the posts, winning the game for the birds.

And this is why the alligator has a big dent in the middle of his nose—because of the time that the eagle landed on it in a ballgame.

Rabbit and Wildcat *(Natchez)*

As Rabbit hopped down the path one morning, he saw a wildcat approaching from the other direction. Rabbit looked this way and that, wondering whether he should run away, but it was too late: Wildcat had already seen him.

"Good morning, Wildcat. I hope you had a fine breakfast before you set off down this path," Rabbit said.

Wildcat replied, "Well, no. As a matter of fact, I haven't eaten all day." He stared pointedly at Rabbit and licked his chops.

"Oh, dear. That's bad. One shouldn't start one's day without breakfast," Rabbit said.

"No, indeed."

"I think turkey makes an excellent breakfast, don't you?"

"It certainly does, but where are you going to get turkey hereabouts?"

"I know where there's a flock of the fattest turkeys you've ever seen," Rabbit said, "and I also know an easy way for you to catch one for your meal. All you have to do is lie down here in the path and pretend to be dead. I'll bring the turkeys to you. You won't have to do a thing except lie there with your mouth open, and when a turkey gets close enough, you bite, and there is your breakfast!"

"Very well. But if you're tricking me, I'll have rabbit for breakfast instead," Wildcat said.

"No, no, it's no trick. Now hold still. I need to make you look like you're actually dead."

Rabbit got some crumbs of rotten wood and put them all over Wildcat's face to make it look like the flies had already been there and laid their eggs on his carcass.

"There. Now you look really dead. Hold still. I'm going to get the turkeys now," Rabbit said.

Rabbit hopped down the path until he came to the place where the turkeys were scratching for grubs.

"Hey, turkeys!" Rabbit shouted. "Have I got some good news for you! You know that wildcat that keeps eating you all the time? Well, he's dead! He's dead, and his body is just up the path there. Let's all go and have a dance to celebrate. You can dance around him, and I'll sing for you."

The turkeys whooped for joy and gladly followed Rabbit down the path.

There Wildcat lay, not moving a muscle.

"He really is dead!" one of the turkeys said.

"Yes, he really is!" Rabbit said. "Now, how about that dance?"

Then Rabbit began to sing:

Catch that big old turkey!

Catch the one with the red head!

Catch the one with the big tail!

"Hang on a minute," the turkeys said. "Are you sure that's the right song?"

"Very sure. I mean, Wildcat is dead, and he can't hurt you, right? I think it's the perfect song for the occasion," Rabbit replied.

Rabbit kept singing as the turkeys danced round and round Wildcat.

Sometimes Rabbit would say, "Now how about you jump on him? He can't hurt you! It'll be fun!" and the turkeys would jump on Wildcat's body.

Wildcat lay ever so still throughout all of this until, finally, one turkey came just a little too close to Wildcat's open jaws.

Snap!

Wildcat's sharp teeth closed over the turkey's neck, and all the rest of the birds flew away in fright.

Wildcat stood up and looked around for Rabbit, but Rabbit was nowhere to be seen. As soon as Wildcat had caught his meal, Rabbit had run away just as the turkeys had done, and so managed to live another day.

The Sky Maidens' Canoe (*Alabama*)

There once was an Alabama village close to a river. The people were accustomed to seeing canoes being paddled up and down the river by people going fishing or visiting relatives in another village, or taking items to trade elsewhere.

One day, something happened that they had never seen before: a canoe came floating down from the sky instead of down the river. The canoe was full of young women, and when they had beached their craft on the riverbank, they all got out and began to play a game of ball. The people of the village watched in astonishment, not knowing what to say or do. After a time, the young women tired of their game. They got back in their canoe and pushed it out into the water, but instead of floating down the river, it floated back up into the sky.

Now, seeing a canoe full of young women come down from the sky is wondrous enough when it happens once, but the young women kept coming back. For several days, they floated down in their canoe, played a game of ball, and then went back home up into the sky. One of the young men of the village watched the young women the entire time they were there, and soon he fell in love with one of them and decided that he must have her for his wife.

The next time the sky maidens arrived in their canoe, the young man hid in some bushes near the place where the young women played ball, and when the one he desired got close enough, he jumped out of the bushes and grabbed her. When the other maidens saw what had happened to their companion, they ran back to their canoe in fright. They sailed back up into the sky, leaving their friend behind.

"Don't be afraid," the young man said to the maiden he had captured. "I'm not going to hurt you. I love you, and I want you to be my wife."

And so, the young man married the sky maiden, and in time, they had several children together. The young man made a large canoe to hold his growing family and a smaller one to use when he went hunting.

One day, the children said to their father, "We are so very hungry. Can you go hunting for us? Bring us back a fine, fat deer to eat."

The man went out hunting, but he returned without having caught anything.

The next day, the children again asked their father to go hunting and bring home a deer, and again the man went out into the forest. This time, as soon as the father had gone, the sky woman gathered all her children and put them into the large canoe. She got into the canoe next to her children and began to sing her magic song, which made the canoe rise into the air. The father heard the song and recognized it. He rushed home and grabbed the canoe, pulling it back down to earth.

When the father went out hunting again, the sky woman put all her children into the large canoe and then got into the small one herself. She began to sing her magic song, and the canoes began to rise into the sky. The hunter again heard the song and ran home, but this time, he could only catch the canoe that had the children in it. The one with the sky woman continued floating up into the air until it was lost from sight.

Many days passed. The children often cried for their mother, and the father missed his wife.

Finally, he asked his children, "Can you sing the sky song your mother sang?"

"Yes, we can," the children replied.

"Good. In the morning, we will all get into the large canoe. We will sing the sky song, and hopefully, it will take us up to the place where your mother is."

When the sun rose, the man and his children got into the large canoe. They sang the sky song, and the canoe began to float up into the air. The canoe rose up and up until, finally, it came to the land above the clouds.

The man and his children got out of the canoe. They began to walk toward a nearby house, where an old woman sat just outside the door.

"Welcome," the old woman said. "Why have you come here?"

"My wife is here and has been here for many days. My children miss their mother and would like to see her again," the man said.

"Yes, you may see her again. She is just over there. She spends her days singing and dancing. But you have had a long journey and should eat before you go to her. Please, sit down, and I will bring you a meal."

The man and his children sat down, and soon the old woman brought out a single cooked squash.

"I don't think that's going to be enough for all of us," the man said.

"Never fear. There's always plenty when I make a meal."

The man and his children ate the squash, but they were still hungry. Lo and behold, another cooked squash appeared in the place of the one they had eaten! The man and his children ate that squash, too, and another, and another until they were so full they could not eat another bite. After the squash was all gone, the old woman brought the family some corn, but they did not eat it. Instead, they went to look for the sky woman and took some of the corn with them.

They walked until they came across another house.

The man asked the person who lived in the house, "Where is my wife and my children's mother?"

"She is just over there. She is singing and dancing," the person replied.

No sooner had the person said that than the sky woman came dancing past, but she did not recognize her husband and children. The next time she danced past, the children took some of the corn and tossed it at her, but although she still paid them no mind, she did smell the scent of the corn.

I know that scent, she thought. *That's like the corn I used to eat when I was on earth.*

The third time she danced past, the children tossed corn at her again, and this time, she noticed them. She ran to her husband and children and embraced them with great joy. Together the family got into their canoes and went back down to their home near the river.

For a time, the sky woman was happy living with her husband and children, but she missed her sky home very much.

Finally, she went to her husband and said, "I love you, my husband, but I cannot stay here. The sky is my home. My children and I belong there. Tomorrow we will be going back, and we shall not return."

The husband was very sad, but he knew it would be wrong to force his wife and children to stay. In the morning, they said tearful goodbyes to one another. Then the woman and her children got into the large canoe, which floated back up into the sky when the woman sang her magic song.

For a long time, the man was sad because he missed his wife and children. However, eventually, he married another woman from his own people, and they lived happily together for many years.

The King of the Tie-Snakes (*Creek*)

One day, a village chief summoned his son to him.

The chief handed the boy a beautiful clay bowl and said, "My son, take this to the chief of the village to the north, and give him a message that I will tell to you. The bowl will show the chief that you are my son, and you speak for me."

The chief told his son the message, and the boy left on his errand.

On the way, the boy came to the banks of a river, where some other children were throwing stones into the water. Wanting to join in the fun and not thinking about what he was doing, the boy threw the bowl his father had given him into the water, where it promptly sank.

Oh, no! the boy thought. *I can't complete my errand without that bowl, and I surely can't tell my father what I just did. What shall I do?*

After a moment's thought, the boy decided to dive into the water to see whether he might find the bowl. The water was very deep; the boy swam down and down and down without reaching the bottom, and the further down he went, the darker it got.

Finally, he reached the riverbed and began feeling around with his hands, trying to find the bowl. He had not searched for long when he felt his arms and legs enwrapped by writhing, slimy creatures. He had been captured by tie-snakes!

The tie-snakes brought the boy to an underwater cave. In the cave was a tall dais, and at the top sat the king of the tie-snakes.

"Climb up to the top," the tie-snakes said to the boy.

The boy put his foot onto the base of the dais but recoiled when he found that it was made of a mass of writhing tie-snakes.

"Come on, climb up to the top!" the tie-snakes repeated, so the boy tried again.

It was very difficult to find places to put his hands and feet, and the surface of the dais kept shifting with the writhing of the snakes, but finally, he made it to the top.

"Come and sit near me," the king of the tie-snakes said. When the boy was seated, the king added, "Look over there. There's a beautiful feather hanging from the roof of my cave. It's yours if you can hold onto it."

The boy went over to the feather and put his hand around it, but it slid out of his grasp. He tried again, and again the feather slipped away. The boy kept trying, and on the fourth attempt, he held onto the feather.

The king of the tie-snakes pointed to a tomahawk in another corner of the cave. "You can have that, too, if you can hold onto it."

The boy went to the tomahawk and tried to get hold of it, but it slipped out of his grasp. He kept trying, and on the fourth attempt, he was able to hold onto the tomahawk.

The king then said to the boy, "You must be my guest for three days. After that time, you can go back home, but on no account must you tell your father where you have been or what you have seen. When he asks you, you must say, 'I know what I know,' and nothing else. But if your father needs my help, you may tell him that you know how to get that help for him, and this is what you shall do: At dawn, walk eastward with the feather and tomahawk and bow three times toward the rising sun. When you do that, I will send aid to your father."

The boy spent three days among the tie-snakes, and on the third day, they brought him back to the place where he had dived into the water. The tie-snakes gave him back the bowl, which he carried along with the feather and the tomahawk from the tie-snakes' cave. The boy swam back to dry land and ran home to his father, who had given his son up for dead.

"Where have you been? We all thought you had drowned in the river," the chief said.

"I know what I know, but if ever you need help, the king of the tie-snakes has offered his assistance to you," the boy replied.

For many days, the chief and his son lived peacefully among their people, but there came a time when a messenger arrived saying that a neighboring chief was planning an attack on the village.

The chief said to his son, "I think now is a good time to ask the king of the tie-snakes for help."

"I will go at sunrise. That is what I was told to do," the boy said.

In the morning, the boy took the feather and the tomahawk and walked eastward. He bowed three times to the rising sun, and when he stood up after his third bow, there was the king of the tie-snakes.

"You have summoned me. What may I do to help you?" the king of the tie-snakes asked.

"Another chief is preparing to attack our village. Can you help us defeat our enemies?"

"Yes. Tell your father that all will be arranged and that he will be victorious," the king of the tie-snakes replied.

The boy went home and told his father what the king of the tie-snakes had said.

That night, the enemy chief and his warriors launched an attack on the village, but they did not get far. The chief and his people didn't even know there had been an attack until they went outside and saw the enemy warriors lying on the ground, all tied up by tie-snakes.

The chief of the village and his men took the enemy's chief and warriors prisoner. The two chiefs talked together and made peace, so the tie-snakes let the other warriors go to their homes unharmed and slithered back to their home under the river.

The Owl Bridegroom (*Caddo*)

Once there were twin girls whose ambition was to marry a powerful chief. They always kept their ears open for news, and soon they heard that a powerful chief lived nearby and that he was unmarried.

The girls went to their parents and said, "We want to go to the village of that powerful, wealthy chief and see whether he will take us as wives. May we go?"

The parents gave their blessing, so the girls set out on the road to find the village they had heard about.

They had traveled some way when the first girl said, "I wonder how far it is to that village. We have been walking for a long time and have not seen anyone."

"Yes," the second girl said. "Maybe we should ask for directions. Let's keep going this way, and if we come across anyone, we will ask."

The first girl agreed that this was a good idea, and so the two girls resumed their journey. It wasn't long before they saw a man carrying a turkey in one hand walking down the path toward them.

The girls greeted him and said, "We're looking for the village of a powerful and wealthy chief. We want to be his wives. Would you happen to know where that village is?"

Of course, the man had no idea what village they were talking about, but they were both beautiful girls, so he wanted them to be his wives.

"Well, today you are in luck! I just so happen to be that chief. I'm here on the road because I've just been to a big council. Very important. It's the kind of thing I do—I'm powerful, and all the other chiefs respect me. I would certainly like to have you both for my wives, but first, I need to go home and consult with my grandmother," the man said.

The girls thought it odd that a powerful chief would need to ask his grandmother's permission to marry, but they agreed to wait until he returned.

Now, this man was no chief. He was simply Owl.

He ran home and told his grandmother, "We need to clean the house, quickly! I have met two beautiful girls who think I am a powerful chief, so they want to marry me. If we do things right, we can fool them."

Owl and his grandmother put the house to rights, and then Owl hung the turkey he had caught from the rafters.

"Here is what we will do with the turkey. In the morning, ask them which turkey you should cook for us to eat. Pretend to point to one in a different part of the house. I'll tell you to cook this one that I just hung up. It will make the girls think that we always have plenty of food," the man said.

Owl went back to the place where the girls were waiting and took them back to his home. He introduced them to his grandmother, and when the girls saw how nicely the home was kept, they agreed to marry Owl and live with him.

Now, every day afterward, Owl came home with a turkey, which he claimed to have hunted. But this wasn't true; in fact, he was going to the council of a powerful chief every day. The chief sat on Owl's back during the council and paid Owl for his trouble by giving him a turkey.

After a time, the girls began to tire of eating nothing but turkey.

"I wonder whether our husband really does go hunting every day," the first girl said.

"Yes, it does seem strange that he never brings home anything but turkey. Let's follow him tomorrow and see where he really goes," the second girl said.

In the morning, Owl left the house and headed for the council place as he usually did, and the girls followed behind him as stealthily as they could. They waited in some bushes when Owl went into the council house, and when they thought it was safe, the girls crept up to the door and peeked through the crack. There they saw their husband, with the powerful chief sitting on his back! The two girls were so shocked they screamed.

Owl recognized his wives' voices and stood up in alarm, throwing the chief down to the ground. Owl then ran home and shouted at his grandmother for letting the girls out of her sight.

For their part, the girls felt ashamed at having been fooled so badly, so they returned to their parents' home, where they told their mother and father everything that had happened.

Kutnahin's Gifts

A time came when a group of young men decided to see whether they could walk to the place where the sky meets the earth.

"Maybe we can even get into the sky country!" one man said.

"Yes! I've always wondered what the sky country is like," another said.

So, the men set out on their journey. They walked to the north for many, many days until finally, they reached the place where the sky meets the earth. There they found the sky rising and falling. Each time it rose, a path to the sky country was opened, but when it fell, it came down very, very fast. The young men decided that it was worth the risk to run under the sky when it opened. They waited until the time was right and then ran as fast as they could through the gap. Unfortunately, only six of the men were fast enough to get all the way through; the others were crushed when the sky fell back down.

The men traveled through the sky country until they came to the home of Kutnahin.

"Welcome. You can stay here as long as you like," Kutnahin said to the men.

After many days in the sky country, the men decided that they wanted to go back home.

Kutnahin asked them, "In what form would you like to return to earth?"

"I'd like to be a squirrel, please," the first man said, so Kutnahin changed him into a squirrel.

The man tried to jump from the sky down to the earth, but it was too far a distance. When he hit the earth, he died.

Kutnahin asked the next man what form he would like to assume. That man also chose an animal form and died when he plummeted from the sky to the earth.

Another man tried his luck as an animal, and he also died.

When Kutnahin asked the fourth man what he would like to become, the man said, "Change me into a spider."

Kutnahin granted his request, and so the man attached one end of his silk line to the sky and carefully lowered himself down to the earth.

The fifth man asked to be made an eagle. He spread his wings and glided down from the sky.

The sixth man said he wanted to be a pigeon. He also flew down safely to earth.

Now, not only had Kutnahin changed the forms of these men, but he had also given them special gifts to share. To the man who became a spider, he gave knowledge of healing songs and dances. This man became the first healer, and he taught what he knew to the people of his tribe. But a sorrowful thing had happened while that man was visiting Kutnahin. One of the people of his village died before the spider came back down to earth, so the spider could not heal him. This is how death came to the world.

The man who came back as an eagle showed the people how to catch fish, and the man who came back as a pigeon showed the people how to grow corn. The gifts of these men meant that the people would always have good things to eat.

The Girl and the Panther (*Creek*)

In a village near a river lived four brothers and their little sister. Not far from their village lived Istepapa, the panther, whose name means "man-eater."

One day, Istepapa was paddling his canoe down the river and happened to pass by the girl's village. There, he saw the girl, who was drawing water from the river.

Istepapa guided his boat to the riverbank and called to the girl, "Come and take a ride in my canoe!"

"Oh, no, I mustn't. I've heard stories about men like you. I won't get into your canoe," the girl replied.

"All right. But what if I told you I have a basket full of panther cubs here? Would you like to see them?"

The girl hesitated, but she did love baby animals, so she got into the canoe. No sooner had she sat down than Istepapa pushed off from the riverbank and paddled down the river as fast as he could toward his home. The girl screamed for help, but all her brothers were out hunting, and the other people of the village were too far away to hear her.

When Istepapa got home with the girl, he gave her to his wife and said, "Here. Look after this girl. See that she does not run away."

In the morning, Istepapa got ready to go out hunting. He said to his wife and the girl, "I expect you to be ready to cook dinner as soon as I get home. Make me soup from acorns and meat. Find the acorns and wash them well in the stream."

Then Istepapa left the house.

The wife said to the girl, "Oh, it is most unfortunate that you are here. You should know that if my husband comes back without any game, he takes a chunk of my flesh to eat. I'm sure he'll do the same to you if you don't get away."

"How can I escape?" the girl asked. "I don't even know where I am or how to get back to my village."

"I will help you. But first, we'll gather some acorns. Then we'll ask Kotee the frog to help us."

The girl and the woman gathered acorns and went to the riverbank. There, they found Kotee.

"This girl is in trouble. Will you help her?" Istepapa's wife said to the frog.

"Yes, indeed I will. What must I do?" Kotee replied.

"Take these acorns. When Istepapa returns, he will ask whether the acorns have been washed. You must tell him no."

"Very well. I will do that."

Then the wife turned to the girl. "It's time for you to go. Run away as fast as you can. Follow the river upstream, and you should come to your village. Always run! Istepapa surely will come after you, and you need to get home before he catches you."

The girl thanked the wife and then ran off up the riverbank as she had been told to do.

When Istepapa got home, he said, "Little girl, did you wash my acorns?"

Kotee replied from the riverbank, "No."

Istepapa was puzzled. He heard the voice, but couldn't see the girl.

So again, he asked, "Little girl, did you wash my acorns?"

And again, Kotee replied, "No."

Istepapa went down to the riverbank—since that is where the voice seemed to be coming from. Seeing Istepapa approach, Kotee jumped into the water with a splash.

"Aha! You can't get away from me that way!" Istepapa said.

He dove into the water where he had heard the splash, thinking that the girl was trying to escape by swimming. Istepapa dove down under the water, but he could not see the girl anywhere. He surfaced and looked up and down the river but still did not find the girl.

Istepapa went back home and took out his magic wheel that could find anything he told it to find. Istepapa threw the wheel in one direction, but it came right back. He tried another direction and another, but each time the wheel returned. Finally, he tried the direction in which the girl's village lay, and the wheel did not come back.

Istepapa followed the wheel, and soon he began catching up to the girl.

He could hear her voice singing as she ran:

I have to reach my brothers' house before they catch me.

I have to reach my brothers' house before they catch me.

Now, the girl had nearly reached her brothers' house, and her youngest brother heard her song.

He went to his elder brothers and said, "I hear our sister's voice. I think she's in danger. Let's go help her."

The brothers all went out of the house and stood listening. The sound of their sister's song was even closer now.

They heard her singing:

I have to reach my brothers' house before they catch me.

I have to reach my brothers' house before they catch me.

"Yes, that is our sister," the elder brothers said to the youngest. "We're going to go help her, but you stay here. You're too young for this task."

"I am not too young. I'm coming, too, and you can't stop me," the youngest brother said.

The four brothers ran toward their sister's voice.

Soon they saw their sister running toward them, and not far behind her were the wheel and Istepapa. The girl ran past them and straight into their house. The elder brothers all shot arrows at the wheel and Istepapa, but they missed. Then the youngest brother took the paddle that he used for preparing food. He ran up to the wheel and smashed it with the paddle. Then he ran up to Istepapa and struck him a great blow on his head, killing him instantly.

"It's a good thing you came with us. We all surely would have died but for you, and you saved our sister," the elder brothers said.

Here's another book by Matt Clayton that you might like

Free Bonus from Captivating History (Available for a Limited time)

Hi History Lovers!

Now you have a chance to join our exclusive history list so you can get your first history ebook for free as well as discounts and a potential to get more history books for free! Simply visit the link below to join.

Captivatinghistory.com/ebook

Also, make sure to follow us on Facebook, Twitter and Youtube by searching for Captivating History.

Bibliography

Brown, Virginia Pounds, and Laurella Owens, eds. *Southern Indian Myths and Legends.* Birmingham: Beechwood Books, 1985.

Bushnell, David I., Jr. *Native Ceremonies and Forms of Burial East of the Mississippi.* Washington, DC: Government Printing Office, 1920.

———. "Myths of the Louisiana Choctaw." *American Anthropologist* n.s. 12/4 (1910): 526-35.

———. *The Choctaw of Bayou Lacomb, St. Tammany Parish.* Washington, D.C.: Government Printing Office, 1909.

Curry, Jane Louise. *The Wonderful Sky Boat and Other Native American Tales of the Southeast.* New York: Margaret K. McElderry Books, 2001.

Dorsey, George Amos. *Traditions of the Caddo.* Washington, D.C.: Carnegie Institute, 1905.

Eastman, Elaine Goodale. *Indian Legends Retold.* Boston: Little, Brown, and Company, 1919.

Grantham, Bill. *Creation Myths and Legends of the Creek Indians.* Gainesville: University Press of Florida, 2002

Lankford, George E. *Native American Legends: Southeastern Legends—Tales From the Natchez, Caddo, Biloxi, Chicasaw, and Other Nations.* Little Rock: August House, 1987.

Macfarlan, Allan A., ed. *Native American Tales and Legends.* Mineola: Dover Publications, Inc., 1968.

McKee, Jesse O., and Jon A. Schlenker. *The Choctaws: Cultural Evolution of a Native American Tribe.* Jackson: University Press of Mississippi, 1980.

McNeese, Tim. *Illustrated Myths of Native America: The Northeast, Southeast, Great Lakes and Great Plains.* London: Blandford, 1998.

Peterson, John H., Jr., ed. *A Choctaw Source Book.* New York: Garland Publishing, Inc., 1985.

Swanton, John R. *Source Material for the Social and Ceremonial Life of the Choctaw Indians.* Washington, D.C.: Government Printing Office, 1931.

———. "Animal Stories From the Indians of the Muskohegean Stock." *Journal of American Folk-Lore* 26 (1913): 193-218.

———. "Mythology of the Indians of Louisiana and the Texas Coast." *Journal of American Folk-Lore* 20 (1907): 285-89.

Thompson, Stith. *Tales of the North American Indians.* Cambridge, MA: Harvard University Press, 1929.